T0120366

ALSO BY TOMÁS Q. MORÍN

POETRY

Patient Zero

A Larger Country

NONFICTION

Let Me Count the Ways

AS EDITOR

Coming Close: Forty Essays on Philip Levine

AS TRANSLATOR

The Heights of Macchu Picchu by Pablo Neruda

Machete

Machete

××× POEMS ×××

Tomás Q. Morín

ALFRED A. KNOPF
NEW YORK
2024

THIS IS A BORZOI BOOK PUBLISHED BY ALFRED A. KNOPF

www.aaknopf.com

"Life Preserver" is translated from the Spanish of Javier Velaza, "El Salvavidas," *Los Arrancados,* Editorial Lumen, Barcelona, 2002.

LIBRARY OF CONGRESS CATALOGING-IN-PUBLICATION DATA
Names: Morín, Tomás Q., author.
Title: Machete: poems / Tomás Q Morín.
Description: First edition. | New York: Alfred A. Knopf, 2021.
Identifiers: LCCN 2020057342 (print) | LCCN 2020057343 (ebook) | ISBN 9780593319642 (hardcover) | ISBN 9780593319659 (ebook) | ISBN 9781524711986 (trade pbk.)
Subjects: LCGFT: Poetry.
Classification: LCC PS3613.07542 M33 2021 (print) | LCC PS3613.07542 (ebook) | DDC 811/.6—dc23
LC record available at https://lccn.loc.gov/2020057342
LC ebook record available at https://lccn.loc.gov/2020057343

Cover design and illustration by Bráulio Amado

Manufactured in Canada
First Edition Published October 12, 2021
First Paperback Edition, July 23, 2024

for

Jack

Dios aprieta, pero no ahorca.

God squeezes, but He doesn't strangle.

—SPANISH PROVERB

Contents

I

I Sing the Body Aquatic

When I offer my sweaty hand in greeting
I can see the future. No matter
how gently you squeeze, I know
when our hands meet you will crowd
my crooked index and pinkie fingers
against their straight-as-an-arrow brothers
so that my hand looks more like a fin
than an appendage perfectly evolved
for tying shoelaces or wiping a tear
from the red face of the missionary
who rode his bicycle under the sun
all day to reach my porch.
When he takes my hand he won't find hope
or brotherhood or whatever
he's looking for. Because I can see
the future at times like this
and because I have an unshakable faith
in the law of averages, I know
when our hands embrace he'll find
proof of natural selection
in the shape of my fingers, evolutionary
holdovers from an era of gills
when the earth was all aquarium
and some distant relative with sleepy eyes
and splayed fins who tired of being mocked
by handsome carp said, *To hell with it*

and climbed out of the sea and across
moonlit dunes toward a sandy life.
In that moment he couldn't have predicted
300 million years later one of his
descendants having long since grown legs
would be belly down on a beach
before an ocean that would carry him
and his own to the land of Montezuma
to roast in the sun for four centuries
where their conversion into dry Catholics
would be so perfect you would never guess
I can't swim to save my life
or anyone else's or that the sound of a wave
pounding a rock makes me nostalgic.
You would never know any of this
until we met on the street
or you knocked on my door and embraced
my hand and felt Galilee on my palm,
which you might mistake for nervousness
unless you were familiar with the embarrassment
of having the only wet fins at a party
because somewhere in your family there was a pike
or two hailing from one of the lost schools
that under pain of death swam
far from the Atlantic or Mediterranean,
around both of which I hear shame
and fear are still the coins of the realm.

112th Congress Blues

Between those symbols of vision the pyramid
and eagle In God We Trust sits in sturdy
caps where it has testified since the 1955
Congress yoked Yahweh to the greenback,
which the nickel would say was about time
because it had been preaching the faith
ever since the last days of Lincoln, though
back then it carried a shield and not
the mug of Jefferson, he of the splendid
mind that cleansed the Gospels of Plato
by that miracle of miracles called reading
until all that was left was a Jefferson Jesus
who was wearing tiewigs when he ascended
to the dome of Monticello from where
on a day without clouds he could see
down from the little mountain past the apple
and peach trees all the way to the debating
loons on Capitol Hill who believed then and now
in evil, that there is a hell with a devil
two shades redder than Oklahoma
dirt, that you can know him by his goat
hoof, or his less famous chicken foot
which you can buy, nails intact, at the grocery store
where they are called chicken paws, not feet,
which is no doubt for the squeamish
who can't bring themselves to eat a foot,

though they have probably chewed
and ripped apart a fried leg or a breast
with such enthusiasm it would make a hen
or two probably faint at the sight and to
the good vegetarians wondering where
is the divine justice in all of this tearing
of flesh they have only to listen to the crunch
of the special recipe skin as it cuts the cheek
and gums of my brother carnivores
just enough for one of my kind to yell *Goddamn*
and call up his state rep, who knowing nothing
better to do proposes a law that already
exists when he should instead order
a two-piece special with a biscuit
and bleed a little, and run his tongue over it
until he can remember for our country
it's never really been about money
or God but about the pain in which we trust.

Whiteface

1. We drove five miles under the speed limit.
2. We kept the nose of our cars out of crosswalks.
3. We signaled early.
4. In the trunk, the spare was full of air.
5. We made sure we had gas.
6. Running out of gas left a lot to chance.
7. "Don't get stranded," our mothers had always said.
8. In the wrong neighborhood.
9. Or on the highway.
10. Or alone.
11. Or with our friends.
12. Keep both hands on the wheel.
13. "Is your registration up to date?"
14. "Did you replace the bald tire?"
15. "It wobbles."
16. "You know who wobbles? Drunks . . ."
17. We nod and nod.
18. Nodding doesn't comfort our mothers.
19. Not like in the 70s and 80s.
20. We were still children then.
21. We hadn't learned to lie yet.
22. At least not well.
23. Breaking curfew was still in the future.

24. Our mothers wanted us safe.
25. They still believed this was possible back then.
26. They nod and we nod.
27. Our two heads swing back and forth.
28. Like a Newton's cradle.
29. You know the toy, if not the name.
30. It often sits on the desk of people who give orders.
31. Five suspended spheres are lined up.
32. They are made of steel.
33. Lift one and they will click and clack forever.
34. You can see it now, can't you?
35. This toy that proves momentum and energy are not lost.
36. Sometimes only two spheres are used.
37. But our heads are not made of steel.
38. They are made of stardust.
39. Stardust is surprisingly delicate.
40. It is delicate like a trapeze.
41. Our heads swing high in the dark.
42. Our country is a circus tent.
43. The trapeze has always been the last act of the night.
44. This is why we nod and nod.
45. Because we are at the end of something.
46. From down below, when the light catches our heads, they shine.
47. They shine like disco balls.
48. They shine like something sharp.
49. Like a thing that could light your way.

50. That could make your heart race.
51. That could free you.
52. We saw a trapeze act on TV once.
53. Two people passed a ball to each other.
54. It was shaped like the Earth.
55. If the Earth were made of glitter.
56. We wanted a ball like that.
57. So we collected pounds and pounds of empty cans to sell.
58. All summer.
59. Coke, Mountain Dew, Pepsi, Big Red, Crush.
60. Miller Lite and Coors too.
61. Not unlike the ones on the shoulder now.
62. Where we have been pulled over.
63. Because of a phone call.
64. Because a dog crossed the road.
65. Because a diaper needed to be changed.
66. Because the route to the dentist was under construction.
67. We are big.
68. We are small.
69. Our clothes are plain.
70. We are wearing pants.
71. We are wearing a dress.
72. A shirt with sleeves.
73. A shirt with no sleeves.
74. The bullet leaves its jacket on the road.
75. The speedometer squats at zero.

76. Red and blue lights dance in the mirror.
77. What if next time we wore a doctor's coat?
78. Hung a stethoscope around our necks?
79. What if next time we wore our mother's camouflage?
80. We could be the color of sand and rocks.
81. What if next time we wore a black suit?
82. And shiny black shoes.
83. A white priest collar around our throats.
84. When you say, *Showmeyourhands! Getontheground!*
85. We could say, *Hail Mary, full of grace . . .*
86. What if next time we paint our faces white?
87. Like a happy clown.
88. Say we were on our way to wave at kids with our machetes.
89. From the edge of the woods.
90. Near a playground.
91. Near a house.
92. Near a school.
93. This person has the right to remain breathing.
94. Anything they say can and will be used against them in a court of law.
95. They have the right to an attorney.
96. If they cannot afford an attorney, one will be provided for them.
97. Do you understand the rights I have just read to you?
98. With these rights in mind, do you wish to speak to us?

Weather Sayings

Piece by piece breaks   the black wall
cloud of police;   they pound
like rain and say don't   call it pain.

× × ×

The cold fish   and muddy clouds
of your face blacken   then blue.
At work, your friends   clown and tip
toe around   in their rain boots.

× × ×

When hope doesn't   rise like bread,
drink the sunlight   to stay fed.

Machete

When they stare
I know it is my skin

they fear, this face,
this hair so unlike theirs.

I meet their eyes
and make them sway

like fields of cane.
When they stiffen,

I sharpen the edge of my smile
and watch them fall.

I love them
in my cake, how they sink

in the dark coffee
where they give up

the sweetness
they make me take

one slice at a time.

Extraordinary Rendition

FOR PHILIP LEVINE

When the CIA said, *An extraordinary rendition*
has been performed, I knew Lester Young
blowing his saxophone in that way he did
when Billie Holiday was a few feet away
smoking, singing "I Can't Get Started,"
was not what they had in mind. No, the agent
at the lectern talking to reporters
who spends most of his days staring
at computer screens riddled with numbers
and names and maps of places he's never been
probably thought of a man in a hood
far from home swimming
in a room flooded with questions.
If the agent had children
to pick up from school after work
maybe he thought, in spite of his training,
of the hooded man's daughter waking
to find her father gone, her mother
in pieces. What might never cross his mind
is how sometimes that same girl
or any one of a hundred others
might be imagining him
an ocean away, standing in a pressroom
in a charcoal suit, one size too big,
stammering to explain the state
of their nameless fathers one day, the wail

a drone makes the next. In her mind
and language "extraordinary rendition"
still means her mother humming
"Somebody Loves Me" with more heart
than anyone she's ever heard
before or since. If you think the agent
and daughter will meet at the end of this poem
for the first time, then you're wrong
because they met many years ago
when he closed his eyes
and the trumpet she presses against
her lips when she dreams entered his sleep
like a bird made of metal. Hungry
and not sure of what it saw, it plunged
toward the cut-open chest
of our agent (it is always this way
in his dreams) as if diving into a lake
and then soared to a great height
from where it dropped his unbreakable heart
that whistled as it zipped past our windows
just before it hit the sidewalk.
Because this scene will repeat itself
for years, a therapist will one day say *guilt,*
forgiveness, and *pain* to our agent
to unsuccessfully explain how death,
when it comes from the sky, makes a music
so hypnotic you will never forget it,
a truth that has always been obvious
to the daughters and sons of Palestine.

Flea Circus

When everything died a few rejoiced
because it meant losing
the horror of butchering
the last animal for the last
supper of meat. The next time
everything collapsed,

I joined the circus and slept on straw,
read Tolstoy
to the snoring zebras, lectured them
on the holiness
of the haunch, on the hideousness
of tears. Tonight,

I am the star grinning in the center
of the ring, waiting
for the gasp of the first housewife
to see the well-groomed
mat of hair on my back
that will remind her

of the dogs she loved, the ones
she could no longer feed
or bring herself to eat. The lights dim
and I wait on all fours
for the music to cue the girl in sequins
whose job is to pour

along my back the bucket of gymnasts
        and high-wire acts
to make me dance and join the chorus
        with my baritone
until the crowd rises to its feet and laughs
        the stale, heartsick night away.

A Sigh

FOR DAVE LUCAS

In the middle of the road of our life
I wandered upon a dark wood a gloomy wood
a dark wood within a darksome wood
a gloomy wood a wood so drear
a forest dark a darkling wood within
wood obscure gloomy wood
darksome wood a darkling
wood a forest dark and deep
a dark wood through a night-dark
wood within a darksome wood
forest dark shadowy wood
darksome wood dusky wood
a forest in darkness
darksome wood gloomy wood
a darkling wood astray
dark wood dark forest
gloom-dark wood within
dark wood dark wood dark wood
a dark wood unfathomable
dark wood dark woods wood so dark
within a shadowed forest
a great forest bewildered inside
dark wood in a dark wood
wood in this dark wood
dark woods in darkened forests

dark wood dark wood dark
wood sunless wood in a dark forest
dense cage of leaf, tree, and twig
that cut through our way like a knife
and we, we hardly knew the difference.

New Year's Eve

The Racial Dot Map of America
says green dots are blacks, blue are whites,

orange are Latinos, red are Asians, and brown
are Native Americans and everyone else.

If this is what passes for hope
then what are the green dots

between my tulips and the sea?
Maybe somewhere green dots still mean grass.

In America blue dots are an ocean
full of fish with no gills. I need to believe I can breathe

underwater. When you see your reflection in this map,
what story do the dots tell you

about freedom and its promises?
When I look at garland, I now see

the Transcontinental Railroad and the Middle Passage
wrapped around our plastic tree.

The year is late. Tonight the sky will
pop with color and gunpowder. Drums

pound in the distance. The only color unassigned
on the map is white. No people live

where the map goes white.
White is prairie, forest, mountain,

river, and desert. White is where the coyote growls
when we decorate the night sky. White is

where the brush waits for a spark
to burn it all new.

Sartana and Machete in Outer Space

FOR JESSICA ALBA & DANNY TREJO

There has been so much death. So much killing.
From space, the wall along the Rio Grande
isn't even a shadow of a shadow.

The rockets of his jetpack are cold now.

His mamá named him Isador Cortez.
México renamed him Machete.
                    a.k.a. Navajas. a.k.a. Cuchillo.

Isadoros is Greek for "gift from Isis,"
the goddess who took the shape of a scorpion
and healed the sick and raised the dead.

How can I explain the man behind the legend?
Not everything people say is true.

For one, he never joined ICE.
He was no good at following orders
anyway, and yet, on Sunday mornings,
while I slept, he'd stalk the neighborhood
for pan dulce and barbacoa for tacos,
        not too oily, not too dry.

To the ladies my papi is puro catnip, a sabertooth bone,
a walking Juan the Conquer root.
Even the Selena statue whistled at him

when we drove to Corpus
so I could show him how to fish.

When he was born, God said,
you will be a Mexi-can, not a Mexi-can't.

He finishes rewiring the navigation system of a nuke
he's sitting on and winks at me. Outer space is cold. Colder
even than the day he thought I was killed.

We didn't know the villain of the month
had messed around with clones,
so while I was held captive on a space station,
my poor Machete put my double in the ground,
Agent Sartana Rivera,
while twenty-one guns saluted her.

What did my man find when he followed the bad guy
into space? Hundreds of kidnapped immigrants
forced to build a space station at gunpoint.

240,000 miles above the Earth
and it's the same old shit as down there.

Can you believe Cortez means "polite"?
I lost count of how many bad guys
he's killed. He doesn't even know.
When I asked him once, he said,
Machete don't count
and then laughed so hard

I thought the sombrero of the woman
tattooed on his chest was going to fall off.

Life hasn't been all bad. He did find me here in space.
You could say our love is galactic now.

He's only a cucuy to the pendejos
who see gardeners, busboys, and maids
when they look at us. What I see
is not God's scorpion or a hurricane of blades,
but the man I love riding a nuclear missile like a Harley
into the mouth of a black hole.

He's like a chromed-out star that forgot how to fall.

I know when my papi lights up the sky
in a few minutes, people are gonna talk
and say all the babies born today
were born under a bad sign.
The blister on my heart
and this machete in my hand say different.

Stanza

Because in medieval Italian it meant "room"
I tied the curtains at their elbows with
what could have been honor cords or worse
yet, a belt from the 60s, so hideous were the
tassels that were dancing a little tarantella
after I had propped the windows and the wind
had carried in the song the rubbing trees
were making, without any accompaniment,
mind you, from a tambourine, although the bells
of the occasional sleigh played that part,
while I waited for the vixen and their shameless
yelping to follow the music and the cold
and the night inside where I sat half man,
half snow, to investigate my squeaking
pencil and the flapping of the bird-white page
I couldn't seem to catch in those years when I
lugged around a frozen heart and was infatuated
with whiteness, since I had read somewhere it was
the absence of color, which could not be true
since I had once loved a pure white duck with
a white bill and feet and I had even torn its white
flesh with my teeth that were still then white,
which should have been all the proof anyone needed
to debunk our outdated theories of absence.

Life Preserver

It's not pointless to love,
                                        finally.
Just like training snakes, it calls for
a refined technique and losing our shame
of performing in front of the world in loincloths.
And nerves of steel.
                                But loving is a job
with benefits, too: its liturgy soothes
the idleness that maddens—as Catullus knew—
and ruined the happiest cities.
Under the tightrope there stretches—don't ask
for a net, it's not possible—another rope,
so loose,   but ultimately
                so pointless at times,
below which there is nothing.
                                                And half-open
windows that air out your anger and show
to your night other nights that are different, and like that
only love saves us at last from the grip
of the worst danger we know of:
to be only—and nothing else—ourselves.
This is why,
                    now that everything is said and I have
a place in the country of blasphemy,
now that the pain of making words
from my own pain
                                has crossed the thresholds

of fear,
    I need from your love an anesthetic;
come with your morphine kisses to sedate me,
come encircle my waist with your arms,
making a life preserver, to keep the lethal weight
of sadness from drowning me;
come dress me in the clothes of hope—I almost
had forgotten a word like that—,
even if they fit me big as on a child
wearing his father's biggest shirt;
come supervise my oblivion and the gift of unconsciousness;
come protect me—my worst enemy
and most tenacious—, come make me a haven
even if it's a lie
                —because everything is a lie
and yours is merciful—;
                        come cover my eyes
and say it passed, it passed, it passed,
—even if nothing passed, because nothing passes—,
it passed,
      it passed,
            it passed,
                  it passed.
And if nothing will free us from death,
at least love will save us from life.

Translated from the Spanish of Javier Velaza

II

××××××××××××××××××

Vallejo

You can't just sneeze anywhere anymore.

I was pushing you in the stroller when the sidewalk ended
like a roll of floss. I crossed the street
and the old woman walking her Jack Russell
                    said, "Oh, you didn't need to cross!"

If she had heard one of my monstrous sneezes,
followed by your mama saying, *Vallejo!*
would she have thought it also sounded
like I was saying the name of the poet?

I swear he looks like a young Abraham Lincoln
in the sketches of Picasso.

I need some human poems today.

Human poem sounds odd, unlike the *Poemas humanos*
of César Vallejo. That's a title people can get behind.
I asked the English language if we could do any better—
it shrugged its shoulders
          and said, *people poems, mankind poems*?

There are too many dogs in this neighborhood.
Where are all the cats?
A day with a cat is a master class

in keeping your distance
from even the ones you love.

My cat was 19 years, 10 months, and 3 days old
when she died. At least that's the story I tell
since really all I ever knew was the birth date
of her two kittens.

She'd be aces at all this "stay home,
wash your hands often" business.

I wish she was still here
so I could show her the video
of the swans and the dolphin swimming
in the canals of Venice.

Sure, a Smarty Arty proved they were fake.
I guess for some people only real hope
has value during an apocalypse.

I keep thinking about the old woman and her dog.
I hope she's okay and doesn't think
I was afraid of her. Can you imagine that?
All it took was a pandemic to turn the world
into a pineapple upside-down cake.

The virus kind of looks like one, to be honest.

Just a block later, I pulled a rose petal
and let you smell it. I smelled it first,

to show you how. I know you smiled,
but maybe it was because I looked so happy
breathing that pink petal in so deep.
When you opened your mouth,
I said *no-no-no,* but I hear
some fancy humans do eat roses.

I love you, but can you take your sister
and please slip away from gravity
in the flying saucer of your Baa Baa black sheep?

I don't want you to see the planet this sad.

Tell him to fly around the Earth
as fast as Superman did in 1978.
Your mama was the age you are now
when that happened. Looking back,
that time doesn't seem so bad anymore.

Tell him to fly counterclockwise
because the future waits in that direction.
You'll like it there—it's safe enough
that a dish can still run away with a spoon.

Two Dolphins

Because the instructions
had only pictures,

I put the crib together
in half the time.

Have I told you
how lost I feel,

how words confuse me
when they sit limp

like a water hose with no water
on a sheet of directions

next to words? I'm so
disoriented right now

by the imaginary
sheet of words

I just invented
that six lines ago

I wrote "next to words,"
when what I meant

to write was "next
to pictures." And even

the whole business
of that water hose

simile is odd,
but not in the good way,

and now I'm noticing
that it's also phallic,

and thinking "Jeezuz H."
can a man for once

not include a penis,
real or figurative,

in a poem with breasts?
Let me try again;

I put together the crib,
changing table, rocking

chair. I hung the *Life Aquatic
with Steve Zissou* print

perfectly level. I keep
the twin bed neatly made

with its melon and mint
blanket and its rows

of marching elephants.
I know how to *do*

these things. I can even change
diapers, dress my son,

bathe, feed, and burp him,
not in that order

necessarily, but I'm open
to things changing

weekly because they do
and have and will.

Tonight, when I said
to his mama

that she should sleep
all the way through

if she wanted to
because I would wake

when he did, I thought,
"I got this."

I said it deadpan,
as is my way

when I want to get a laugh,
when I pretend

to be the tough hero
who sacrifices something,

only I never am.
I'm the character who clowns,

the one who loves
etymologies so much

that after he learned
the pan in deadpan is slang

for the face
googled "words for

a man's chest"
only to lose hours

in the list
of questions under

<u>People also ask:</u>
What is a Man Boob?

Is a tank top tan line
called a double dolphin?

How Big Should
male nipples be?

What's another word
for treasure chest?

What is the synonym
of honest?

Do men's nipples leak?
If a man is a rooster

does he have breasts?
Thoughts like these

keep me up watching
the monitor.

When it wails,
I hurry down the hall.

Clean diaper?
Check. Food, burp?

Check, and check.
So we bounce

on the exercise ball
that is blue like the ocean

in some Japanese paintings.
I used to spend

so many hours
on this ball

trying to tighten my abs
and obliques

—riblets, I called them.
He fusses and wiggles

while the Glo Worm
curls in a corner

with Brahms and
other classics

deep in its body
waiting to be released.

I stop bouncing and tilt
the ball forward

and back to rock us.
From the changing table

the velvet blue face
of his Twilight Turtle

watches me;
the smile it wears says

it could live forever
in this room,

forever throwing
a field of orange stars

and crescent moons
from its back

onto the ceiling
and walls.

Our rocking syncs
with the sound machine.

I picked OCEAN
because to my ear

it was the least threatening
of the six choices.

THUNDER means lightning
has already struck

somewhere or
someone. WATERFALL

is Annie Taylor in 1901
tumbling in a barrel

down Niagara Falls.
RAIN is a leaky roof.

SUMMER NIGHT
is crickets and no wind

or electricity to run
the box fan.

And RAINFOREST
is the *chip chip tweet*

of birds near and far,
a pleasant chorus

that'll put me to sleep,
which is a clear

and present danger
to us both. So OCEAN

it is: surf, gulls,
a sandpiper.

This was my lullaby
when my parents

brought me home
from the hospital

to their tiny apartment
on North Beach.

Across the street
the piers and the gulf

where my father
caught lunch

and dinner for them.
What do sand

and infinite water
look like in the dream

of a child who's
never seen either?

I drop my shoulder
and now the baby

is at a 45 degree
angle. He's the hypotenuse

that closes my triangle.
His open mouth

brushes my nipple
and pinches it

for only a second,
but it's long enough

to startle me
from my nocturnal

daydream
of dunes and the

damp sunlight
of the beach. He misses

his mama's body
that is resting

all night
for the first time

in weeks. I press
the soft back

of the pacifier
against my nipple

and he gets to work,
his little fingers

kneading my chest
like dough

—my son the poet
already mixing

metaphors
out of my body.

Who could blame him.
During the day

my skin is a desert.
My chest is two palm trees

and the distance
between them a mirage.

But tonight
my body is a boat

named the *Belafonte.*
My breasts are two dolphins

with electronic gear
strapped to their heads

who stare with goofy grins
when they're asked

to do something
simple like swim

under a hull
and send back footage.

My heart wears
a pale blue uniform

and a red knit hat
because my heart

is Bill Murray
playing a famous

oceanographer.
Using a cross-section

model to give a tour
of the boat,

his voice-over
is clear and dry

when he says, *This is*
the observation bubble,

which I thought up
in a dream, actually.

Two albino scouts
swim with the ship.

They're supposedly
very intelligent,

although I've never seen
any evidence of it.

Royal Silence

FOR C. DALE YOUNG

This much I know, as I came down the mountain
and the valleys were revealed and my ears
clogged so that all I could hear was the inside
of my own head, I became a brother for a while
to the nineteenth-century hunter who dressed
in that green between olive and ivy, the one the Jets
still wear, though they haven't been in the hunt
since Broadway Joe wore pantyhose for Beauty Mist
or danced around the Orange Bowl like a buck
in rut darting and dodging across a field of blue
daisies in late fall, a dumb creature to be sure
for all its nobility, and I probably couldn't
ever shoot one, not that I've tried, besides
someone said you shouldn't carry loathing
in your heart when you aim at a deer or a grouse
or a bear, which it would pain me to do,
especially the bear, who can sound like a Hare Krishna
when he's happy, his head bobbing, every huff
and grunt in a clear timbre, except when he's angry,
the bear that is, his pitch is closer to a bull's
or a bullfrog's, a bull bullfrog declaiming
in a Polish accent that silence is royal,
and natural, and that the world only speaks
when we have committed a sin or two
against it—this is an old ribbit, he says, retold
over and over through history; think Memphis

and Rwanda; think Chile and Warsaw; think
New Delhi and Granada where that romantic
disciple of everything green who is dead, who was shot,
that sleepless King of the pond, still croaks
into the green wind “Verde que te quiero verde”
loud enough to wake the dead and keep them so.

Goosestep

A collector of walks, I was practicing my llamastep
when one of those white geese with the knob
of cheddar on its bill honked at the goslings
ignoring the art of the rank and file so adored
by Mussolini and other assorted lunatics
who I have trouble believing could ever raise one leg
parallel to the earth they scorched without falling
prey to gravity that was given a special kind of dominion
over the fascist paunch, a shabby thing
I have never seen hang around the waist of a goose,
though who can say for sure under all that heavenly
down where the hips of a goose begin and end; and even
if tomorrow some budding scholar published a treatise
titled *The Mystery of Goose Hips* to fanfare,
it would be an exaggeration of the grossest kind
to equate a goose's trumpet with the barking
from the balcony by the sad bullies whose love
of the locked leg I will never understand
since the knee was so obviously made to flex,
which means locking one is most likely a kind of sin
against Darwin or God, both of whom I think
would disapprove of anything so unnatural
as even twenty people moving in stiff unison
to music unless the brass and strings
were just about to sway and bend to the hot
version of "When the Saints Go Marching In."

A Pile of Fish

FOR PAUL OTREMBA

Six in all, to be exact. I know it was a Tuesday
  or Wednesday because the museum closes early
on those days. I almost wrote something

  about the light being late—; the "late light"
is what I almost said, and you know how we
  poets go on and on about the light and

the wind and the dark, but that day the dark was still
  far away swimming in the Pacific, and we had
45 minutes to find Goya's *Still Life with Bream*

  before the doors closed. I've now forgotten
three times the word Golden in the title of that painting
  —and I wish I could ask what you think

that means. I see that color most often
  these days when the cold, wet light of morning
soaks my son's curls and his already light

  brown hair takes on the flash of fish fins
in moonlight. I read somewhere
  that Goya never titled this painting,

or the other eleven still lifes, so it's just
  as well because I like the Spanish title better.
Doradas is simple, doesn't point

out the obvious. Lately, I've been saying
dorado so often in the song I sing
to my son, "O sol, sol, dorado sol

no te escondes . . ." I felt lost
that day in the museum, but you knew
where we were going having been there

so many times. The canvas was so small
at 17 x 24 inches. I stood before it
lost in the beach of green sand and

that silver surf cut with pink.
I stared while you circled the room
like a curious cat. I took a step back,

and then with your hands in your pockets
you said, *No matter where we stand,*
there's always one fish staring at us.

As a new father, I am now that pyramid
of fish; my body is all eyes and eyes.
Some of them watch for you in the west

where the lion sun yawns and shakes off
its sleep before it purrs, and hungry,
dives deep in the deep of the deep.

Heretic That I Am

Three days now the mold
has advanced across the face
of the peach I caught
with one hand like Willie Mays,
saving it from the sidewalk
and its army of black shoes
and how could it happen
that my peach turned
into Castro, the young one
who regularly baptized
the microphone and the first row
of sleepy workers with his spit
and anger and love. What is love
if not a commitment to fatigues
and I wonder if he wore sea green trunks
to the beach or olive pajamas
with padded feet? I have to know
if mold lived in his crisper too, and did
it goosestep even in that temple
of cleanliness before which he kneeled
and hunted the last rebellious
grape unwilling to bear the tyranny
of vines. This morning I am
the one kneeling and praying
in the kitchen over the beard
of my communist peach, how

it's a second cousin of the hacky sack,
albeit spongier, like a meatball,
which reminds me the letter M
is for Marx, and for moon shot,
and for miracle. And sooner or later,
M is also for mercy, mercy we have
beauty, mercy we can't live forever,
mercy we have time and rot
to work our stubborn flesh away
from the bald, pale soul
that screams with joy when it pops up
and free toward the first night
of October in Indian summer.

Tried and Untrue

I lost a lake once. It had no name. No fish
ever swam in its waters. Starbursts of lilies
never once bloomed there. Along the banks
pine after pine rose as high as houses, but no bird
ever made a home in those branches. The sun
never shone on my lake. I did have a moon,
and darkness, too. But I never made time for stars.
I used to make a game of sitting on the bottom.
When I grew bored of this, I hung in the sky
like a bird with no wings. Or a cloud with no wind.
My lake was made of words, you see.
I was a young man trying to make beauty
out of loneliness, as young men like to do.
When my friend Phil read my lake and said, "Ahhhh,
it's your old tried and untrue lake again.
Get a new lake," I laughed like someone with nothing
to lose for the first time in years. Seventy-one percent
of the Earth is covered in water and more than
half of your body is an ocean. Countless
species become extinct every day, and countless more
are discovered. Both return to and arrive
from a place beyond our knowing
where there are no lakes for the lonely. Pain
is the anchor on a ship with no sails. But in this
here and now, this here of cookouts and frisbees,
rowboats and tackle boxes, every fish
loves the fly more than the shadow of the fly.

Duct Tape

One night I thought, "If only I were thin
and petite as cellophane
they might welcome me in heaven."
Light doesn't pass through
my thick body and no one ever said
I was the life of the party.

Will the saint at the door find my name
on his clipboard? Things fall apart
even in heaven, don't they?
Who better to help the angels
than me—if they truly exist—
when their feathers drop
from flying too little?

I never get these thoughts in the daytime.
The whisper of a new sun
telling the swallows to sing
fills me with hope. Today
a woman took five inches of my life
just as the streetlamps flicked on
and the dogs in the neighborhood yawned.
Tomorrow, the two of us
will hold together a sign
that says THE END IS NEAR.

She wants what we all want.
She sobs softly. When I tear

no one looks for an elephant
in the room—; I am the grand toad
of grief when I split open.

I miss the simple life: kissing
someone's thighs
while they walk down the street
in their torn blue jeans. Or hugging
the hips of a hose
without any worry
I wouldn't be hugged back.

She stares out the double window
she never opens anymore.
The sun is low and turning
into an orange ghost.
Ten years ago next week
we met when she moved in
with the man she would marry
and divorce. I was in his toolbox
but didn't stay there. She let me sleep
next to the glue stick and her
grandmother's pipe
in a kitchen drawer.
You could say I was like the child
they never had.

All these years later
and I'm still useful. Just yesterday,
she made me sing my swampy song

strip after long strip.
When she was done,
I covered the ostrich leather journal
that had been her favorite
wedding gift. The pages were blue
like a robin's egg
but the skin was butterscotch.

When her back hurt, she sat on a pillow
and wrote nothing I could read,
mumbling each sentence
until she sounded like the sea.
Or the leaves of a tall tree
before a storm. I had wanted to listen
to her but kept getting distracted
by the bumps (quill follicles, I think,
is what she had called them).
I was so used to being flat.
Now I felt like a coat
of armor for the only bird to ever learn
that running could be flying.

Miles Davis Stole My Soul

is not entirely accurate because John Coltrane was there,
and Bill Evans too, and I forget who else
because after they finished playing and fled the scene
I felt kind of, not blue exactly, but green,
the kind the old masters used to paint trees groaning
or the warm sheen on a rotten ham. My soul
had begged me to listen to jazz
after we argued about the stoic on the corner
selling flowers, ranting about paradise
and how the soul was a kind of vegetable, a cucumber
I think he said, which I wanted to believe,
even if the cucumber is obviously a fruit.
My soul knew this wasn't right
of course, it being the subject in question,
so it sought to prove me wrong
by inviting Miles and Co., while I was making a salad
no less, two parts radish, one part joke,
to dip their notes like ladles and empty
my heart. By the time I'd chewed the last piece of lettuce,
my soul was gone and there was no one left
with whom to argue about the seemingly arbitrary
best by dates on milk cartons
which are meant to convey a sense of security,
however fragile, or about the defect in every body of water
an impressionist painted, who, for all their love
of nature never set one ripple right,

a fact I learned in the days that followed
searching for my soul in lakes and rivers,
dishpans and aquariums, because God is nothing
if not a comedian, and when I still couldn't find my soul,
I found an intersection and lectured on charity and loss.
I still remember the sweet faces in the passing cars
when I began to pray for rain and dance
the flamenco; I remember it was a Wednesday
because nothing significant ever happens on a Wednesday.

When no clouds bloomed on the horizon
as a symbol of divine forgiveness, I returned home
where I found the stoic with milk on his lips,
skinning an orange, standing in the same place
I had stood with my salad, this peddler of cucumbers
whom I was going to remind about the laws
of property, except he started singing,
yes, singing, a song I hadn't heard before
but that I was sure was godly
because I recognized Galilee and Adam and shame,
as well as the white rolling of his eyes,
which told me he was now a servant of the music
making his throat open and close like a gate,
releasing the warm floodwaters of his voice
that filled and overran the hole
I had still been calling my heart.
If in that moment you had been flying
in a plane high above the country of my body
you would've been surprised, as I am now, by the sight
of barren plains broken by a system of clear lakes

shaped like a patch of wild cucumbers,
a once noble fruit that saved nations
because it was hardy, versatile, and demanded so little.

Machetes

I wrote a poem once
that I called "Machete." It was angry

because I was angry
when I wrote it, angry over

white supremacy
and blah blah blah. It's okay

if you haven't read it
because it only had one machete

in it and everyone knows
a poem with multiple machetes

always trumps
a poem with a single one.

Can we reclaim that word yet?
You know the one

I'm talking about.
Don't make me say it again.

So if you're one of the few
billion people who hasn't

read my machete poem,
the recap goes like this:

a single machete,
gold and shiny,

descended from the Aztec
heaven of jaguars

and naked women
on flea market paintings . . .

That joke was going to be
longer, but I can't

keep a straight face
for more than six lines,

even when the lines
are as short

as these are.
The truth is

that poem was about
weaponizing my smile

by giving it a sharp blade
to slice all the white

supremacists
inside that poem,

the ones who
I made dance

like fields of cane.
Notice how I implied just then

"my poem did this,
and my poem did that,"

instead of saying
I was responsible

for those choices
that felt right, and still do.

That poem does contain one lie
that I feel bad about,

which is silly,
because what poem doesn't

contain a lie or two?
Even so, this one bothers me

so here's my confession:
at the end of that poem

I said that I drink coffee.
I don't. Never have.

Why don't you drink coffee?
people always ask.

I don't like the taste
is what I say, and that,

well, that's a truth
you can carve on my headstone

without disturbing my sleep.
What has kept me up

for months now
is the feeling that I forgot

to put something
in that single machete poem.

I've sat cold in my burrow,
washing my whiskers,

tuning my ears
to the gentle footfalls

of that feeling
that has been stalking me

for days and days.
I didn't know

what it was until I heard
Chen Chen read

in snowy Vermont.
His dark jacket and pants

were pin-striped
like a cage for the soft leopard

shirt he wore.
I don't think

I had seen him
since we had been teammates

for the Poetry World Series
with Erika M.

and even though we won
the game, the real victory

came while we waited,
on the corner of Crosby

and Houston,
for the crosswalk signal,

when he and I decided
we would go west

to Miss Lily's
and the group

could go where it wanted
because we didn't want

a sports bar,
because we didn't want

American food,
because we didn't want

to take orders
from the white woman

we didn't know
who put herself in charge

of the group that night.
Now I'm not saying

she was a white supremacist
but she was wielding

something heavy and blunt
and invisible.

And really, shame on her
for forgetting

that just ten minutes before
our team had bested

that all-star lineup
of Melissa S. and Adrian M.

and Erika S.
after nine close innings.

Couldn't she see
we all had crowns?

Chen, do you remember
how everyone smiled

and said they'd join us
when we said we were going

our own way?
Maybe they tapped

into their inner cats
in that moment

and could smell the jerk chicken
and the fried plantains

already sizzling
a short half mile away.

Do you remember
the size of my eyes

when I whispered
that we had passed

Cuba Gooding Jr.
on the way to our booth?

I know, I know,
Show me the money!

is the quote from *Jerry Maguire*
everyone remembers,

but for me it's always been
the thing Cuba's character says

about "kwan,"
how, *It means love,*

respect, community, and dollars,
the entire package.

And I know if we talk
about kwan in the poetry world

then the dollars part
becomes a punch line,

which is okay,
because laughter is what I forgot

to put in that poem
with the single machete.

You reminded me
anger can also be funny

when I heard you read
that poem about cats,

or was it the one about dogs,
and this was a truth

I had always known,
or at least something I had

known for a very long time
but had forgotten

the day I sat down
to write my smile

into a machete
I could use

against my enemies.
But you and your poems

broke the stillness
of that cold night

in a chapel
I'm not sure

was ever meant
for laughter

and so I stepped
out of my burrow,

smiling, just as I did
this morning

when I woke from a dream
in which I was a house cat.

I was a tortie
and with every step

my legs grew longer
and my shoulders

churned
like the discs of a plow

under my skin
that was now golden

like the color of wet
limestone.

I stretched taller
and longer

until my teeth
and legs and claws,

even my tail
that was now as long as my body,

all felt lethal
like machetes.

I'd forgive anyone
who seeing me like this

said I was a "beautiful
death machine"

like Karen the cougar
in *Talladega Nights,*

a role that was played
by two mountain lions

named Dillon and K.C.
who liked to roll around

in the grass
between takes.

I like to think
"I'm a beautiful life machine,"

but I know
that will be a hard sell

for some readers
because this is now

a poem filled with many machetes
and how can a reader

ever tell when I'm
being angry-funny

or funny-angry
if they won't cast off

their clothes
and embrace that wild

inner-something
that roams inside

all of us and join me
over a pile of spare ribs,

our lips smacking,
stripes of sauce

on our cheeks,
not unlike how it was

in the beginning
for our species

before we had words
for what a life was

or someone to say
we must change it.

Notes

PAGES 3–4

Had my sometimes sweaty hands and feet never been diagnosed as acute hyperhidrosis, I would never have thought to trace my origins back to the sea in "I Sing the Body Aquatic."

PAGES 17–18

I was inspired to compose "A Sigh" by Caroline Bergvall's "VIA." My poem begins and ends with my translation of the famous opening three lines of Dante's *Commedia:*

> Nel mezzo del cammin di nostra vita
> mi ritrovai per una selva oscura,
> ché la diritta via era smarrita.

Here is my translation:

> In the middle of the road of our life
> I wandered upon a dark wood
> that cut through our way like a knife.

I split these three lines in my poem by inserting forty-eight different versions of "selva oscura" by forty-eight different translators. Here are the translators, the years of their translations, and the order in which their versions of "selva oscura" appear in my poem.

> Cary, 1805; John A. Carlyle, 1849; Cayley, 1851; Pollock, 1854;
> Brooksbank, 1854; Longfellow, 1867; Rossetti, 1865; Johnston, 1867;

Pike, 1881; Sibbald, 1884; Minchin, 1885; Wilstach, 1888; Norton, 1891; Musgrave, 1893; Sullivan, 1893; Vincent, 1904; Wheeler, 1911; Chaplin, 1913; Shaw, 1914; Johnson, 1915; Edwardes, 1915; Langdon, 1918; Anderson, 1921; Fletcher, 1931; Binyon, 1933; Bodey, 1938; Sinclair, 1939; Sayers, 1949; Bickersteth, 1955; Foster, 1961; Singleton, 1970; Musa, 1971; Mackenzie, 1979; Mandelbaum, 1980; Sisson, 1980; Phillips, 1983; Creagh and Hollander, 1989; Heaney, 1993; Ellis, 1994; Pinsky, 1994; Arndt, 1994; Dale, 1996; Durling, 1996; Ciardi, 1996; Zappulla, 1998; Schwerner, 2000; Bang, 2013.

The very last line that caps the poem is the only line I wrote. It, and the title, nod to Robert Frost.

PAGES 21–23

"Sartana and Machete in Outer Space" is in the voice of Sartana Rivera, a character played by Jessica Alba in Robert Rodriguez's films *Machete* and *Machete Kills.*

PAGES 45–46

The "romantic disciple" in "Royal Silence" refers to the great Spanish poet Federico García Lorca. "Verde que te quiero verde" is the first line of his poem "Romance sonámbulo."

PAGES 59–71

In the poem "Machetes," the line "*It means love, / respect, community, and dollars, / the entire package*" is a slightly altered quotation from the movie *Jerry Maguire.* The line, as spoken by Cuba Gooding Jr., is "It means love, respect, and community, and the dollars, too. The entire package."

Acknowledgments

My thanks to the editors of the following publications in which these poems appeared.

Academy of American Poets' Poem-a-Day (poets.org): "A Pile of Fish"
The American Poetry Review: "112th Congress Blues"; "Miles Davis Stole My Soul"; "Machete"; "Two Dolphins"; "Machetes"
The Awl: "Extraordinary Rendition"
Blackbird: "I Sing the Body Aquatic"
Boston Review: "A Sigh"; "Whiteface"
The Greensboro Review: "Duct Tape"
Mississippi Review: "Tried and Untrue"
The Nation: "Life Preserver"
New England Review: "Royal Silence"
The New York Times Magazine: "New Year's Eve"
Poetry: "Stanza"; "Goosestep"
The Rumpus: "Weather Sayings"
Slate: "Flea Circus"
The Threepenny Review: "Heretic That I Am"
Virginia Quarterly Review: "Sartana and Machete in Outer Space"

"Stanza" was reprinted in *The Poetry Review* in the United Kingdom.

"Extraordinary Rendition" was chosen for inclusion in, and lends its title to, the anthology *Extraordinary Rendition: American Writers on Palestine,* edited by Ru Freeman.

"Heretic That I Am" was reprinted on *Poetry Daily.*

"112th Congress Blues" was reprinted in *Resistance, Rebellion, Life: 50 Poems Now,* edited by Amit Majmudar.

"Vallejo" originally appeared in *Together in a Sudden Strangeness: America's Poets Respond to the Pandemic,* edited by Alice Quinn.

Gracias to the communities at Texas State University, Drew University, Texas Tech University, University of Texas at Austin, Vermont College of Fine Arts, and Rice University for their support as I worked on this book.

Endless gracias to Deb Garrison for all the care, attention, and love you, Todd Portnowitz & the rest of the Knopf team gave this book.

Gracias y abrazos to my fellow travelers in this beautiful life filled with art: Hasanthika Sirisena, Vievee Francis, Elena Passarello and David Turkel, Patrick Phillips, Courtney Zoffness, Laura Lee Huttenbach, James Arthur and Natalie Diaz, Marie Mockett, Katie Kapurch and Jon Marc Smith, Alan Shapiro, Tom Sleigh, Lauren Berry, Marcus Burke, Lisa Olstein, Melissa Stein, Garrett Hongo, Megan Okkerse, Josh Lopez and Amanda Scott, Carrie Fountain, Sunil Yapa, Elizabeth Schmuhl, Twister Marquiss, David Tomas Martinez, Rowan Buckton, Taneum Bambrick, and Phil Metres and Mike Croley and Dave Lucas.

So many gracias to Erin Evans, Traci Brimhall, C. Dale Young, Micah Larson, Emilia Phillips, Sasha West, Jess Smith, and Paul Otremba, who helped me shape this book, in ways both small and large.

Love and abrazos to my family Rebecca, Chloe, Jack, and the Booms. There isn't a darkness your laughter and love can't slice.

A NOTE ABOUT THE AUTHOR

Tomás Q. Morín is the author of the memoir *Let Me Count the Ways,* from University of Nebraska Press, as well as the poetry collections *Patient Zero* and *A Larger Country.* He is coeditor, with Mari L'Esperance, of the anthology *Coming Close: Forty Essays on Philip Levine,* and translator of *The Heights of Macchu Picchu* by Pablo Neruda. He teaches at Rice University and Vermont College of Fine Arts. Morín lives with his family in Texas.

A NOTE ON THE TYPE

This book was set in a typeface called Baskerville. The face is a facsimile reproduction of type cast from the molds made for John Baskerville (1706–1775) from his designs. The punches for the revived Linotype Baskerville were cut under the supervision of the English printer George W. Jones. John Baskerville's original face was one of the forerunners of the type style known to printers as "modern face"—a "modern" of the period A.D. 1800.

Composed by North Market Street Graphics
Lancaster, Pennsylvania

Printed and bound by Friesens
Altona, Manitoba

Book design by Pei Loi Koay